Grape Growing

A Beginners Guide To Discovering The Fundamentals Of Growing Grapes

Bowe Packer

TABLE OF CONTENTS

PUBLISHERS NOTES

Disclaimer

Kindle Edition 2014
Manufactured in the United States of America

Bowe Packer

DEDICATION

I dedicate this book to all those people out there who remind us of the things we have forgotten about ourselves.

And this holds especially true of my beautiful and amazing wife, Alma. She is the one woman who has the most amazing talent to let me grow and love the things about myself that I have not fully accepted.

I cherish the love she has for me when I may not know how to love myself.

May we all have this kind of beautiful soul in our life.

Sent from LOVE,

Sunshine In My Soul

PART 1: YOUR OWN VINEYARD

STARTING THE VINEYARD

Starting your own vineyard isn't as difficult as you might think. In fact, almost the only thing you need is some land. Now you're probably thinking you need to get the right kind of land but that's not entirely true either. You can grow your own grapes just about anywhere you want and that includes non-traditional areas such as your backyard.

What you do need is knowledge on what to do with your vineyard and how to take care of it properly. You need to know about climate and soil (but you don't need certain ones in order to grow your own grapes).

If you really want to set yourself up for success of course you can look for a great place to start your vineyard. This will be a wide open space (remember vines grow outward and keep expanding) with not a lot of trees or other structures. Too many shadows creates too much room for problems. You don't want your vineyard overrun with mold or fungi which is all too common when you get too much shade overhead. Make sure your area has plenty of sunlight.

WHY BOTHER?

You may be wondering why you should even bother creating your own vineyard. What's in it for you? Well we're definitely glad you asked.

1. For one thing you should know that you would definitely not be alone as a grape producer. Actually many people are beginning to look into this as a viable career option.

2. Larger facilities that produce wine are actually beginning to fall by the wayside. There are fewer of them around and that means that individuals who start their own facilities are doing better. Grape production is down and the market needs more of them. So by jumping into the mix and providing grapes where they're needed you're setting yourself up for success.

3. When you go out into your vineyard you'll find plenty of reasons why it's worth it. Being out in the sun can be a lot of fun and of course you'll be producing excellent quality grapes which is great as well.

4. If you own property already that's only really good for farming then you may want to consider this as well.

After all, you'll be able to make money by planting and selling your own grapes. So you'll be making the most out of your property.

Keep in Mind: It is important to note that you will need to put in some of your own money in order to get anything back from this venture. Make sure you're willing to make that commitment to getting your dreams started.

WHAT YOU SHOULD KNOW BEFORE YOU START?

1. You will need to get involved in the entire process of growing your grapes from the planting all the way through the post-harvest. Don't think you're going to just set someone else up doing all the hard work and reap the rewards for yourself.

2. You're going to want to know at least a little about plant culture before you even put that first seed in the ground.

3. Remember to look into marketing so you know what you're doing once that first harvest gets ready to pull out of the ground. You don't want to harvest your grapes and realize you have no idea what to do with them.

4. If you're planning to purchase a vineyard you'll need to do your research. These can be very difficult to buy because there is such a high demand and most vineyard owners know they can consistently make money this way.

5. The five best markets for grapes are fresh, frozen, grape concentrate, grape juice and wine. Of course

wineries are typically the best in this respect because they are considered the most profitable of all the other options. Make sure you check how things work in your own neighborhood however so you'll know for sure what will net you the biggest profit.

6. Table grapes can be fun and there is a relatively decent market for them. The problem is that the production costs are typically much higher than the costs associated with growing grapes for wine.

SELECTING PROPERTY TO START

Your highly successful, viable market depends on one instrumental starting line, your property. So how are you going to excellent quality grapes? You need to grow the right type for your area. This means understanding what each type of grape needs as far as soil, water and sunlight. There are, after all, going to be a few differences. In general let's get started, after all, most grapes are going to require at least a few things no matter what type you get.

1. Ensure soil will drain properly so too much water isn't pooled at the base of your vines.

2. Avoid extreme temperature zones especially extreme winter temperatures. Moderate temperatures are best because you will be able to grow your grapes without quite so much concern over them freezing.

3. Make sure you have the right level of circulation amongst your grapes. Too little will result in a build-up of fungus and that's definitely not going to be good for your crops.

4. Extreme temperatures or changes in temperature that occur frequently can cause your grapes to become

susceptible to disease. Be careful that you are planting in a typically moderate temperature zone.

5. Plant in a partly-loose soil bed with organic matter so your vines can extend their roots further and continue to grow. This also ensures that the roots will be able to firmly take hold in the ground which makes them less susceptible to wind damage.

THE BEST SOIL

Next you want to make sure you have the right type of soil for your vineyard. You will likely be able to grow your grapes in just about any soil but they won't be quite as abundant or quite as high quality every year unless you keep your soil in the best shape possible. Luckily for you this is a lot easier than you may think. You just need to make sure that you're taking care of it and that you're paying attention to what it needs.

1. Ensure your soil has a moderate fertility level in order to facilitate growing your grapes properly.

2. Make sure there is plenty of drainage both in the soil and on top of the soil so that too much water doesn't stay near your vines and plants as they won't grow properly.

3. The top level of soil, soil that is fertile and good for growing should be at least 30-40 inches deep before you get to a dense level of soil. This is so the roots can continue to grow and push through to the heavier soil.

4. Ensure the soil has at least a small portion of sand content and that it contains a good amount of organic

material. This will help with the growing process and make your vineyard and your grapes even better.

If there is a bad drainage system your soil will not be able to get rid of water and your grapes will not be able to expand and grow as much. You will get a very low yield from your vines and you'll also get a very short lifespan for them as well.

Chemicals properties of your soil:

1. Soil pH level - 5.5 to 6.8

2. Organic matter content - 3%

3. Phosphorous level - 50 pounds/acre

4. Potassium level - up to 300 pounds/acre

5. Magnesium content - up to 250 pounds/acre

6. Zinc content - up to 10 pounds/acre

7. Boron content - 2 pounds/acre

PREPPING YOUR LAND

Some land may prove to be too acidic for growing grapes. This is measured by the level of pH in the ground which can sometimes get to be a little too high. If this is the case, add ground limestone to help reduce the level of pH to neutral or slightly alkaline. These are going to be the best for growing your grapes.

Before you start adding too many chemicals to your soil however, make sure that you are carefully measuring your soil properties. If you don't, you could end up ruining your soil for planting rather than making it better. That's definitely not something that you want to do. So make sure you're decreasing where you should and increasing where you should as well. Some soil will require a little more of certain fertilizers and minerals while others will require less of others.

If you have more than 1,600 pounds of phosphorous per acre you should not add phosphorus for any reason. Really, if you have 300 pounds per acre you should be careful about adding more. This is because phosphorus is not good in too large of quantities for your soil, your crops or the local water table when it runs off with the water. Keep this in mind when you utilize fertilizers containing chemicals as well.

You will need to talk with local authorities to determine the safe levels in your area. This will also help you understand your state's guidelines on chemical fertilizers and chemical levels within the soil that you are using.

In order to fully understand the type of soil that you have you will need to take either a representative sample or a core sample. The representative sample is simply a layer of dirt that is submitted to an agricultural laboratory or experimental station. On the other hand a core sample requires you to dig approximately four inches into the ground. It's recommended that this be done every two years.

ORGANIC FERTILIZERS

If you want to utilize organic methods of fertilizing your property that can be great but remember that organic materials have nutrients in them as well which includes potassium and phosphorous as well as nitrogen. You'll want to understand these so you know what's best for your soil.

Manure Type	Water Content	Nitrogen Content	Phosphorous Content	Potassium Content
Dairy cattle	80%	11 pounds/ton	9 pounds/ton	12 pounds/ton
Swine	80%	9 pounds/ton	9 pounds/ton	11 pounds/ton
Beef cattle	80%	11 pounds/ton	7 pounds/ton	10 pounds/ton
Broiler litter	20%	55 pounds/ton	55 pounds/ton	45 pounds/ton
Broiler layer	40%	35 pounds/ton	55 pounds/ton	30 pounds/ton
Broiler pullets	30%	40 pounds/ton	45 pounds/ton	40 pounds/ton
Goat	70%	22 pounds/ton	5 pounds/ton	15 pounds/ton

Horse	80%	12 pounds/ton	6 pounds/ton	12 pounds/ton
Tobacco stalks	20%	30 pounds/ton	10 pounds/ton	70 pounds/ton

Now remember that organic manure is actually a great alternative to commercial products that many use as fertilizers. That doesn't mean that you shouldn't take care and consider carefully what you're adding into that soil with the manure. For example manure that contains large amounts of certain nutrients can harm the soil for the following year. Keep this in mind when you choose your organic fertilizer.

Another thing to keep in mind with organic fertilizer is what you're getting. Remember you are going to get what animals are producing which means what they are eating is going to be in your fertilizer. Some questions to ask yourself and to investigate further are:

1. What is the livestock eating?

2. What type of livestock is the manure from?

3. How is the fertilizer being stored?

4. How is the fertilizer being handled?

5. When are you applying the fertilizer?

6. How are you applying the fertilizer?

NUTRIENTS NATURALLY FOUND IN MANURE

Some of the most common nutrients you will find are:

1. Molybdenum

2. Copper

3. Magnesium

4. Sulfuric compounds

5. Zinc

6. Calcium

If you complete soil sampling and determine that there is little organic material in that soil (less than 2%) then you will definitely want to utilize organic fertilizers because they are so high in nutrients. Of course you can use cut tobacco stalks to provide nutrients as well. You want to make sure they are harvested and covered quickly however so that they do not leach all of their nutrients out during rainfall.

Bowe Packer

LIMESTONE AND NUTRIENT APPLICATION

Now if you need to change the acidity of your soil then you need to make sure this is done well in advance of your planting. You'll also need to know a little about the grapes that you intend to plant so you know how acidic your fields should actually be.

1.) *American hybrids* - 6.5 during planting, 5.5 to 6.0 during production phase.

2.) *French-American hybrids* - 6.5 during planting, up to 6.0 during production phase.

3.) *European grapes* - no less than 6.0 during establishment, up to 7.0 during production phase.

If you need nitrogen you must ensure that there is no more than 3.7 ounces per one hundred square feet of land or no more than one hundred pounds per acre. This must also be applied during your planting season so that the best results are achieved from your plants.

Finally, ensure that there is at least 120 pounds of magnesium per acre in your soil. This will ensure that there is enough to produce a large crop at the end of the season. Remember that you will need all of these nutrients either before or during your planting season so that the grapes get those nutrients right from the start.

Check out these tables for more information on applying other nutrients and fertilizers:

Amount of Phosphate in the Soil	Amount of Phosphate Needed During Establishment
70 pounds/acre or more	No additional phosphate is needed.
35 to less than 70 pounds/acre	Up to 80 pounds/acre or up to 3 ounces/100 square feet
Less than 35 pounds/acre	80 to 120 pounds/acre or 3 to 5 ounce/100 square feet

Amount of Potassium in the Soil	Amount of Potassium Needed During Establishment
300 pounds/acre	No additional potassium is needed

200 pounds/acre but less than 300 pounds/acre	80 pounds/acre or 3 ounces/100 square feet
Less than 200 pounds/acre	80 to 120 pounds/acre or 3 to 5 ounces/100 square feet

Amount of Magnesium in the Soil	Amount of Magnesium Needed During Establishment
Below 60 pounds/acre	80 pounds/acre
61 to 120 pounds/acre	20 to 80 pounds/acre
120 pounds/acre or more	No additional magnesium is needed.

Finally, ensure there is adequate limestone so that you have approximately a 6.4 pH level.

Water pH Level	Buffer pH of 5.5	Buffer pH of 5.7	Buffer pH of 5.9	Buffer pH of 6.1	Buffer pH of 6.3	Buffer pH of 6.5	Buffer pH of 6.7	Buffer pH of 6.9
4.5	4.50	4.25	4.00	3.50	3.00	2.50	2.00	1.50
4.7	4.50	4.25	4.00	3.50	3.00	2.50	2.00	1.50
4.9	4.50	4.25	3.75	3.25	2.75	2.25	1.75	1.25
5.1	4.50	4.25	3.75	3.25	2.75	2.25	1.75	1.25
5.3	4.50	4.25	3.75	3.25	2.50	2.00	1.50	1.00
5.5	4.50	4.25	3.50	3.00	2.50	2.00	1.50	1.00
5.7	4.50	4.00	3.50	2.75	2.25	1.75	1.25	1.00
5.9	-	4.00	3.25	2.50	2.00	1.50	1.00	0.75
6.1	-	-	2.75	2.00	1.50	0.75	0.50	1.00

If you wish for a 6.6 pH level then you'll need this chart.

Water pH Level	Buffer pH of 5.5	Buffer pH of 5.7	Buffer pH of 5.9	Buffer pH of 6.1	Buffer pH of 6.3	Buffer pH of 6.5	Buffer pH of 6.7	Buffer pH of 6.9
4.5	4.50	4.50	4.00	3.75	3.25	2.75	2.25	1.50

4.7	4.50	4.50	4.00	3.75	3.25	2.50	2.00	1.50
4.9	4.50	4.50	4.00	3.75	3.00	2.50	2.00	1.50
5.1	4.50	4.50	4.00	3.50	3.00	2.50	2.00	1.50
5.3	4.25	4.50	4.00	3.50	3.00	2.50	1.75	1.25
5.5	4.25	4.50	4.00	3.50	2.75	2.25	1.75	1.25
5.7	4.50	4.50	4.00	3.25	2.75	2.25	1.50	1.25
5.9	-	4.50	4.00	3.25	2.50	2.00	1.50	1.00
6.1	-	-	3.75	3.00	2.25	1.75	1.25	0.75
6.3	-	-	-	2.50	1.75	1.20	0.75	0.50

For 6.8 you will need this:

Water pH Level	Buffer pH of 5.5	Buffer pH of 5.7	Buffer pH of 5.9	Buffer pH of 6.1	Buffer pH of 6.3	Buffer pH of 6.5	Buffer pH of 6.7	Buffer pH of 6.9
4.5	4.25	4.50	4.25	4.00	3.50	2.75	2.25	1.75
4.7	4.25	4.50	4.25	4.00	3.50	2.75	2.25	1.75
4.9	4.25	4.50	4.25	3.75	3.25	2.75	2.25	1.75
5.1	4.50	4.50	4.25	3.75	3.25	2.75	2.25	1.50
5.3	4.75	4.50	4.25	3.75	3.25	2.75	2.00	1.50
5.5	5.00	4.50	4.25	3.75	3.25	2.50	2.00	1.50

5.7	5.50	4.50	4.25	3.75	3.25	2.50	2.00	1.50
5.9	-	4.25	4.25	3.75	3.00	2.50	1.75	1.25
6.1	-	-	4.50	3.75	3.00	2.25	1.75	1.25
6.3	-	-	-	3.50	2.75	2.00	1.50	1.00
6.5	-	-	-	-	2.25	1.50	1.00	0.75

PART II: CARING FOR YOUR VINEYARD

PREPPING FOR THE PLANTING SEASON

There are three different phases to your planting prep. These are plowing, sub-soiling and leveling.

1. Plowing-This turns over the soil so that the moist soil underneath is brought to the top and dry topsoil is pushed down a layer so that it can get more nutrients and a little moister as well.

2. Sub-Soiling-This is a breakup of what's called the pan layer of plowed land.

3. Leveling-You need your land to be flat in order for your vineyard to grow properly. So with this method you'll be able to keep it even and go ahead and start your planting.

Make sure that you get rid of any weeds before you start your planting because you don't want these pests getting into your grapes.

- Thistle
- Johnsongrass
- Quackgrass
- Dock
- Brambles
- Black Medic
- Broadleaf Plantain
- Common Purslane
- Dandelion
- Ground Ivy
- Crabgrass
- Mouse-Eared Chickweed
- Prostrate Knotweed
- Speedwell
- White Clover
- Wild Onions

- Wild Garlic

- Yellow Wood Sorrel

- Below-Ground Rhizomes

- Tubers

- Budding Rootstocks

- Budding Tap-Roots

- Above-Ground Stolons

If you have perennial weed pests in your field you will need to make sure you take care of them quickly. You don't want those in your field and you don't want them to keep coming back every year. Treat them with herbicides as early in your establishment phase as possible so the weeds are killed but the chemical fades out before you plant. You don't want to hurt your vines after all.

COVER CROPS

A cover crop ensures that nutrients stay in the soil and that the soil doesn't erode over time. They also help to get rid of a lot of weed and animal pests. Depending on what you're looking to add to your field you'll want to check out different cover crops but the next section will give you a little bit of overview.

TEMPORARY COVER CROPS

If you're planning to adjust the pH in your field you'll want to start with a temporary cover before you put in a permanent cover. One of the best is lime which will help you with the pH balance that you want and need. Next you'll need to test the soil nutrients and add what's needed to get a good balance and then plant something like Sudan grass as a good cover crop. You can actually plant Sudan grass any time up until August so you'll have plenty of time to get your soil ready.

PERMANENT COVER CROPS

Make sure that you plow your soil once more before you plant your permanent crop cover. You'll want to make sure this is done around August to September so that your cover crop grows in properly.

If you're looking to use fescue or perennial rye as a permanent cover crop you will want approximately 80-120 pounds per acre of field. This will cover an entire floor of your vineyard so that your plants are protected. You can do this through the use of drop-seeding (usually done in late summer).

Next you will want to engage in soil cultivation. This is typically easiest to do when it is hot outside because your soil will be dry and loose rather than moist and packed like it is in the wetter or colder months. Approximately 14 days before you plant your vines make sure you're killing off your cover crops. This is done through the use of systemic herbicide. Be sure you complete this 14 days prior to planting your vines as this gives sufficient time to get rid of the herbicide but not enough time for weeds to grow in.

Next ensure that you completely till the land and that you plant in between your cover crop rows in areas called 'killed rows.' This is the safest and healthiest place for your crops and it's where they'll grow the best.

DESIGNING CAREFULLY

So at this point you must be sure you've completed all of the following steps:

1. Soil sampling

2. Adjustment of pH levels

3. Adding necessary nutrients

4. First tilling

5. Sub-soiling

6. Leveling

Once this has been done you need to design your vineyard. Keep in mind:

1. You want to maximize the amount that you can get per acre with the least amount of time being spent.

2. Optimize your production.

3. Keep your soil safe from erosion.

4. Increase efficiency of your management.

5. Utilize farming equipment to help with your vineyard.

GENERAL GUIDELINES

Make sure that you carefully and clearly draw out the plan for your vineyard before you start making any changes. You need to make sure you plot out tool sheds, storage sheds, roads and all of your rows. Make sure you also block it off into smaller 'blocks' which can be done with professional surveying.

Keep some space on the outside of your vineyard that is at least one row wide so you can easily travel through. Each 'block' should also have wide alleys for travel and to improve circulation. Without circulation your crops won't grow properly and you won't get very many of them either.

POSITIONING THE ROWS

You need to make sure that your rows are facing the right way and that they are getting enough sunlight. You also need to ensure that there is not too much wind coming through your vineyard as this can cause damage to your crops. Another problem can be the steepness of your vineyard as this can cause your crops to wash away if there is too much rain.

You want your rows to run from north to south so that they

can get the best amount of sunlight. You don't want to get too much shade because this will cause trouble for your plants. If you have too much shade then you can space your rows close together and they can run from north to south as well. If the rows are too far apart you'll have more of a problem with shade.

If there is a lot of wind in your area you want your rows to be running parallel to the wind. Don't put them perpendicular as this will cause them to become damaged when the winds kick up. Keep in mind however that a raisin vineyard will need to be arranged from east to west instead of north to south. This will give the grapes more sunlight which they will need for drying.

You will want ideal row spacing rather than adjusting based on your specific vineyard size or farming equipment. Your vineyard will outlast your equipment so make sure you're keeping with existing spacing.

ROW SPACING PROPERLY

You want to install proper trellising throughout your vineyard. Rows of between nine and twelve feet are typically the best. If you have a large slope in the land you'll want to establish larger gaps instead. If you're using different methods of planting you may want to utilize larger gaps as well.

Be sure that you are using the right row spacing. This is going to have a lot of impact on your production and the yield that you get from your vineyard. If you have too wide of spaces you'll have less produce per acre. There are two factors you need to consider for this.

1. The productive rigor of grape cultivar.

2. Expected size of vines at maturity.

Spacing properly ensures that you get the most produce out of your vineyard. Too much space will cut down on the amount of produce you'll get while too little spacing will lead to shade as the vines grow too large for the area. You need to ensure that you're letting the vines have enough space to grow.

Every foot of grape vine can support approximately eight grape buds however this can have a negative effect on them during the winter. These vines may also have lower juice quality if they have too many buds per foot. Remember that lower juice quality means less profits for you. Your grapes will be less marketable.

If you use American hybrid of American-French cultivars then you will want your vines kept eight feet apart. This provides better quality yields. Remember that you'll need average climate conditions. Eight feet by nine feet or 605 vines per acre are average for this type of vine.

On the other hand if you use European grape cultivars you want approximately seven feet between vines instead of eight. These vines will generally have a spacing of seven feet by eight feet or 778 vines per acre.

If you're looking to get the best harvest you want to have at least six hundred vines for every acre of land. This will ensure that you get a quality result and a quality harvest.

Vineyard Layout

Many vineyard owners will tell you that your layout should be rectangular rather than square because it will provide for several advantages based the number of vines able to be planted and the ability for longer rows. Longer rows means that your heavy farm equipment doesn't need to turn or more as much as with square vineyards.

Understand that with rectangular vineyards you'll want heavy soils with load-bearing rows of up to 700 feet long. With drip irrigation you only want rows up to 600 feet. On the other hand if you have sprinkler irrigation you can actually have rows up to 1,000 feet long. Make sure however that you have a heavy enough weight-bearing row to support the different lengths of rows.

Installing a Trellis

The trellis system helps your vines grow the right way. It will train the vines to move the way they need to and it will also keep them up off the ground. You definitely don't want that in your vineyard.

1. Make sure you plant your vineyard before you install your trellis system. You'll also want to wait until your vines grow at least two to three feet and then you can attach them to the trellis.

2. You will need large posts and you will also need post markers throughout the vineyard to keep it going.

3. Hydraulic augers should be used to install the posts. They should be approximately 3.5 inches by 8 feet and they should be at least 2 feet down into the dirt.

4. You want to make sure the grape vines are matured at least slightly so that you can install the trellis. You want the posts between the vines and across rows so that they avoid harming your plants.

5. In between your killed rows is likely not going to be tilled this means you should use pilot holes to help with installing the posts.

6. Use pre-marked sticks to measure that the holes are the right sizes and posts are the right lengths as well.

7. Your vertical posts should be installed across rows first and then make sure you have the H-braces prepared

properly. You want to use the same types of posts for these and drill holes into the ends. You want the holes to be approximately 2.5 inches deep and approximately 3/8 inch around.

8. You want to mark your drill bit to keep the hole only as deep as you need it. You don't want them any deeper. You also want to make sure you put in the same holes in your installed poles.

9. Put 5 inch brace pins into the vertical poles only halfway and then use them to attach the H-brace. You'll want to drill 4.5 inch holes into the outside of vertical posts and then put in 9-inch brace pins. Next you'll want to use the rest of the pins for bracing wires.

10. Splice your bracing wires to create loops. You want those loops running from the top to the bottom of your posts. Ensure that the loops are secure with staples but make sure they're strong enough to hold those metal wires.

11. Once you've completed your anchor system you need to install wire on the top. This is a high tensile wire and should be attached with crimping sleeves which will lock them in.

12. One high-tensile wire should be on each row and it should be attached with at least two staples in every space that you have to attach the top wire to a post.

13. Make sure you put in strainers between your anchor systems as well.

14. A gauge will help you to measure tension on your top wires to keep it just right.

15. Tie strings around the wires to connect them with bamboo supports so the vines grow up.

VINEYARD CARE BY MONTH

MARCH-PRUNING

During the summer you want to ensure that you are completing the proper care.

1. Repair your trellis including wires, posts, etc.

2. Check the tension of all of your wires. Cordon wires should have a tension of 250 pounds or more while high-tensile wires should be at least 300 pounds.

3. Check for damaged posts so that you can remove them and replace them with healthier posts.

4. Prune vines if necessary. You don't want to prune them if you don't absolutely need to as this will negatively affect your harvest.

5. Conduct a thorough soil analysis every two years so that you know what you're going to need as far as nutrients.

6. The table below will help you with some of the particulars of pruning:

Percentage of Primary Bud Mortality	What To Do
0% - 20% mortality	The current pruning technique is working well and should not be adjusted or changed.

| 20% - 80% mortality | Retain a larger number of buds to compensate for the large mortality of early buds. |
| More than 80% mortality | Actively growing nodes should be retained. Nodes should be pruned away *only* if the growth will be pushing against the adjacent grape vine. |

APRIL-VINE PROTECTION

1. This is when you're going to get more trouble with pests and weeds. You need to use herbicides in order to take care of these pests at this point in time. Remember that if you use the herbicide too early in the year you'll have trouble getting it to work properly. Too late could hurt your crops or reduce the abilities of the herbicides.

2. If pruning needs to be done then you can do so in later April because this will result in lower levels of breakage for the buds.

3. Utilize dormant fungicides at this point of the year to ensure that your crops will be healthy later on. You want to make sure your vines have the right amount of sun and circulation as well.

4. You may want to install a fence around the field to keep animals out. Whether you electrify the fence or not is up to you.

5. Make sure that you get debris removed from the vineyard. You want to keep your pruned pieces of the vine out of the field to keep the area clean and healthiest for your vines.

6. If you've lost vines you may want to plant new ones.

7. Check for any kind of pests or bugs and treat these troubles.

MAY-PEST/FERTILIZER MANAGEMENT

1. At this point you want to add in nitrogen if your soil needs it. You may want to complete a new experience at soil sampling so you can check the nitrogen levels.

2. Watch out for different types of fungus and disease during this time of year.

- *Phomopsis (*a fungal disease)

- *Powdery mildew* (a fungal disease)

- *Black rot* (may be caused by bacteria or fungi)

- *Downy mildew* (caused by parasitic microbes)

3. Remember pests are around at this point in time as well. So check for these common types of pests:

- *Cane borers*

- *Phylloxera*

- *Cane gallmaker*

- *Cane girdler*

Understanding more about these pests will help you. So here's a little more information you may need to know.

Cane Borer:

-attack leaves of vines

-appears slightly metallic

-may be approximately 3 inches long

-young borers are larvae with flat heads

-these bugs lay their eggs before the winter comes and hatch in spring when they grow.

-These leave very characteristic marks

on your vines.

Phylloxera

-These attack the roots of your grape vines.

-These will kills grape vines within months.

-These bugs are quite small in size

-These attack mainly European cultivars rather than the American ones. You can utilize American stock instead if you would like to avoid the problem later on.

-Typically this type of insect will attack in California though it has been found in South America as well.

Cane Gallmaker

-Often found in eastern and Midwestern United States

-Large gallmakers will be approximately 3 millimeters in length and resemble weevils.

-Often these insects will lay their eggs in the winter and their eggs will hatch in approximately the spring.

-These insects will lay eggs only on

vines that are at least 25 centimeters or 50 centimeters.

-Adults will damage the shoots and they will start feeding on the vines themselves.

-Look for swelling shoots or exit holes in the vines as a sign of these pests.

Cane Girdler

-These pests affect young shoots and can even destroy entire grape productions.

-These typically started feeding on Virginia cultivars however they have begun feeding on others more recently.

-Shoots will bend and break when they are infested with these insects. Look for shoots that appear to be pruned in a rough way.

4. Make sure you utilize herbicides during this time of year. You'll want to make row by row checks to ensure that you get rid of the dangerous insects.

5. Water sprouts need to be removed from vines. You don't want your vines to grow one on top of the other and this can happen if the water sprouts are attached. It's a good thing because it means that your plants are healthy.

6. Make sure you complete your shoot thinning at this point as well. You'll want to get rid of any shoots that are undesirable or that you don't need. You want to get rid of anything that isn't growing properly or that has any sign of diseases and pests.

Thinning out the shoots will have benefits such as making your shoots hardier and helping them to grow hardier fruits as well. You'll also be able to reduce the instances of disease. You will also want to make sure there is a watering spray and herbicide applied regularly.

7. You'll want to use cluster thinning to increase grape cluster sizes.

8. Make sure you get your shoots narrowed to a narrow canopy by tucking in or using catch-wires.

JUNE/JULY-PEST MANAGEMENT

1. Pest management needs to be done continuously but in June you should look for something known as Botrytis blight. This is a type of gray mold and it occurs typically when there is rainy or cool weather.

In order to see these you will want to check the buds and fruits for mold. You'll want to get rid of any dead parts of your plants as quickly as possible. If your plants have this problem you'll want to take steps to resolve the problem.

-Misting foliage

-Syringing

-Overhead watering

Make sure you have enough spacing and air circulation to help reduce chances of molds of different types. If you can't control your mold problem this way you'll want to get a fungicide. You'll need to be careful to pay attention to what can be used on grape vines so you don't end up hurting your plants.

2. Check for other pests as well, including:
   -Grasshoppers
   -Sphinx Moth
   -Leafroller
   -Leafhoppers
   -Japanese Beetle
   -Rose Chafer
   -Eight Spotted Forester
   -Grape Berry Moth

3. Keep following weed management and protecting your

plants throughout the month.

4. You'll want to check your harvest at this time of month as well. You can multiply the number of grape clusters by the weight of those clusters. This is the time when you can talk with potential buyers and possibly locate someone to purchase your crop.

5. Thin out the leaves of your plants to ensure they get the right amount of sunlight. You'll want to do this when there are fruits already set on the plants.

6. At this point your vineyard may attract animals. You want to ensure that you install bird netting over your grapes and get rid of your cover crop.

7. If your grapes grow early in the year you can have the opportunity to harvest some of them at that point in time and then can sell them earlier on.

8. Vegetation should be allowed at this point in time.

AUGUST-HARVEST SEASON

1. This is the time you're going to get all of your crops out and you'll be selling them off. You want to make sure you're sampling your grapes throughout this time

so you know when they're going to be best for harvesting. Also make sure that you are conducting your Brix measurements at the same time. Inform your buyers of when you'll be ready to sell your harvest.

2. Next you need to make sure that you have freezing and transportation prepared for your harvest. You will need to have them frozen in tubes or fresh when you deliver to the winery. Some of them prefer fresh but they will generally not have trouble with the frozen variety either.

3. Make sure that all of your containers are sanitized thoroughly so that you can ensure that your grapes will be fresh and won't cause any problems.

4. This time of year you'll only really have to worry about grape berry moths and Asian lady beetles.

5. If you seem to have slow maturing grapes then they're probably late-season. Don't worry about them in the least because this is entirely normal. All you need to do is keep following the Brix level and wait for at least a 3 before you harvest.

6. Keep conducting plant and soil analysis throughout the entire harvest season including after the grape blooms.

SEPTEMBER-POST-HARVEST

1. If you have those late-season grapes we mentioned then this is when you're going to be doing your harvesting. You'll want to keep an eye on them at this time.

2. Watch for Asian lady beetles during this month as they become a threat to your harvest throughout this season.

3. Make sure that you remove your bird netting during this month as well.

4. Check for powdery mildew which shows itself as gray or white powder on the leaves of the vines. If you have other crops as well as grapes you will see this powder on those plants as well which usually attacks during the late-harvest.

   It's important that you treat this quickly with a fungicide that is sprayed directly onto all of your plants. Don't only spray the ones currently infected as you could lose other plants as well. There is a special fungicide specifically for this problem in grape vines so make sure that's what you're getting. Treat your plants as soon as you know there is a problem.

5. Herbicides can control the pests and weeds that you may have during this time of year.

6. If you have dry soil make sure that you're using proper irrigation techniques so you don't end up with hard soil caps.

7. Utilize organic fertilizer to replace the nitrogen that has been used up by the vines from that year. You'll use the soil sampling you've been conducting to determine how much and what type should be used.

OCTOBER-PLANNING

1. During this month you want to reduce tension on your wires and repair anything in your trellis system that needs it.

2. If you have an electrified fence you can turn it off at this point since your harvest has been brought in and you don't need to worry about foragers.

3. Drain out your irrigation system.

4. Make sure you get a good idea of what your buyers thought of your cultivar and whether they are interested in purchasing next year as well. You want as

much feedback as you can get. Next look at what they say and what you can do better so you know what to do the next year.

5. Now it's time to start planning the next year's crop.

PART 3: CHOOSING YOUR GRAPE

CULTIVARS

GUIDELINES FOR SELECTION

You will need to know the type of grape cultivars that you want to produce in your vineyard. Some vineyards produce types for white wines or red wines and you'll want to know what you're doing right from the start. You will also want to know a bit about the different cultivars so you know what you can expect when you plant them. Some, after all, will prove more successful for you as a seller than others will. Asking yourself some simple questions can help you to have that success.

1. What is in demand? Think about what your area needs. Does your area need more wine grapes or is that market fully saturated? If there is a need then what particular kind is needed? You are going to want the best profit you can get so think about what your area is going to need come harvest time.

   Once you have a market you'll be able to narrow down the specifics that are necessary for your grapes. These are things that wineries are going to pay attention to and therefore they're going to be very important to you as a wine grape grower.

   > -Color of the grapes
   >
   > -Aroma
   >
   > -Sugar content
   >
   > -Acidity level
   >
   > -Seedless or non-seedless

   Each of these characteristics are going to be important to a winery because they allow the winery to know what they can do with those grapes and what they will produce. They will help you to determine if this is the right grape to be growing.

2. Look toward the future of your market area and think about what will be needed then rather than focusing only on the immediate time. You'll want to know what other vineyards are doing as well as what type of market expansion may occur.

3. Look at your vineyard itself. Different types of soil, weather conditions and wind will be impossible for you to change which means that certain types of grape cultivars will grow better or worse in that environment. Don't try to grow something that simply can't survive in your area, instead, work with your conditions.

4. If you know the growth potential of the grape cultivar that you're looking to plant you'll be able to create a better vineyard design than if you don't because you'll know the right row spacing and trellis system as well. This will improve your production numbers to as high as they can get without hurting your grapes.

5. You'll want a plant that can withstand the winter temperatures in your area. If it gets very cold then you'll need vines that are quite hardy while milder climates may be able to choose more fragile vines. You want to minimize the amount of damage over the winter season.

6. If you wish to plant grapes that don't normally grow in your area you will have higher operational costs which is something you will need to carefully consider. It is not practical, for example, to grow *vitis vinifera* in a vineyard in the Midwest because it does not grow well there and extra work is necessary to keep it alive in the cold climate.

7. There are many different cultivars that you can use if you live in the Midwest:

   - Catawba-This is typically a table fruit so you wouldn't want to grow it in a winery vineyard. The berries are large but have small clusters. They are also a late-season cultivar so you'll get your harvest later on in the season. If you follow proper pruning and maintenance and watch out for downy mildew and fungal diseases you'll have a large harvest at the end of the season.

   - Concord-Usually utilized for fruit juice and wine these grapes have seeds and also are prone to developing black rot. You'll need to follow a systemic herbicide program in order to keep them safe while they are ripening.

- Delaware-This will produce a 'blush wine' for those wineries that specialize in sparkling wines. It also produces a large yield at the end of the season.

- Niagara-This is a very versatile grape which means it can be used as a table grape, a wine or a fruit juice. They have loose clusters and few berries per cluster but produce excellent grape juice and wine.

- Cayuga White-These produce a perfect white grape with high vigor which are used to create a dry wine.

- Chardonel-These are not the grapes used in Chardonnay though they are related to those varieties. They have few grapes and typically produce only a moderate yield during harvest but they are quite resistant to fungal problems.

- Marquis-With a cordon system this cultivar seems to flourish and produces a high-yield cultivar though it is for table grapes and not wine grapes.

8. A cultivar is not the same as a species. So your grapes, cultivar could be one of a hundred contained within one single species of grapes.

GRAPE SPECIES/CULTIVARS

This table will help you understand more about the different species and cultivars of grapes that you will encounter as well as some important characteristics.

Species of Grapes	Popular Cultivars	Native Regions	Characteristics & Vineyard History
V. vinifera	Chadonnay White riesling Pinot blanc Pinot gris Gewurztraminer Muscat ottonel Sauvignon blanc Comtessa Morio Muscat Noblessa Semillon Siegerrebe Cabernet sauvignon Cabernet franc Merlot	This species originated from Asia Minor	The European grape species is popular with vineyards in the Western United States. However, this species (and all its cultivars) are generally prone to attacks from the phylloxera pest. This is the

	Limberger Gamay noir Trollinger Rotberger Petite Verdot		reason why this species is not very popular in the Northeast. *V. vinifera* grapes have longer growing seasons than other grape species and require a hotter temperature in order to thrive. It does not produce high yields if the region is generally rainy during the months when the grapes are ripening.
V. rotundifolia	Triumph Black beauty	All Southern regions of:	These ten species are

V. acerifolia	Taraheel	- Delaware	highly adapted
V. angulata	Black fry	- Illinois	to very humid
V. cordifolia	Tara		areas.
V. hyemalis	Bountiful	Northeast	
V. incisa	Sweet Jenny	Texas	While this is an
V. muscadina	Chief		advantage to
V. mustagenesis	Supreme	Success in	vineyard
	Cowart	growing these	owners living in
V. peltata	Summit	species have	the native
V. verrucosa	Darlene	also been	regions of these
	Sterling	noted in	species, all are
	Dearing	Washington	quite
	Scuppernong	and Oregon.	susceptible to
	Delight	California is	winter injury
	Regale	also a good	(mainly, frost).
	Dixie	place to plant	
	Pineapple	these grape	The lowest
	Doreen	species.	temperature that
	Noble		these species
	Florida		can tolerate is
	Nesbitt		zero degrees
	Florida Fry		Fahrenheit. If
	Magnolia		the temperature
	Loomis		drops to about -
	Fry		10 degrees
	Jumbo		Fahrenheit,

	Higgins Janet Hunt Ison		widespread winter injuries will occur throughout the vineyard. All the cultivars of these species fare well in areas where there is well-drained soil and swamps. Though these species can tolerate hot summer months, the vines will not grow well if exposed to semi-arid conditions.

			Unlike *V. vinifera* and all its cultivars, these species are immune to attacks from phylloxera and even nematode invaders.
V. labrusca *V. blandii* *V. canina* *V. ferrunginga* *V. latifolia* *V. luteola* *V. sylvestris virginiana* *V. taurina* *V. vin. sylvestris americana* *V. vulpina*	Alexandar Himrod Champion Reliance Concord Niagara Delaware	Can be found in northeast regions and east regions of the United States.	All species and cultivars from this line of grapes are also immune to phylloxera attacks. The *V. labrusca* species has been used for many years to produce hybrid grapes that are resistant to pests.

V. aestivalis *V. nortoni* *V. lincecumii* *V. bicolor*	Norton Americana	These species can be found in numerous ranges, from the northern hemisphere all the way to the continent of Africa.	It is said that these species are immune to Pierece's disease, a devastating condition caused by bacterial pathogens that are spread mainly by the insect pest *leafhopper.* One of the negative traits of these species is that they generally do not produce hardy root systems.
V. riparia *V. amara* *V. callosa*	Riparia Martin, *et. al.*	These species and cultivars are widely	These grape stocks have been known to

V. colombina *V. concolor* *V. cordifolia* *V. cordifolia riparia* *V. dimidiata* *V. illinoensis* *V. incisa* *V. intermedia* *V. missouriensis* *V. montana* *V. odoratissima* *V. palmata* *V. popufolia* *V. rubra* *V. tenuifolia* *V. virginiana* *V. virgniensis*	(No English counterparts to the original French names of these grape stocks have been created)	distributed throughout the states in the US. From Tennessee to Manitoba, to the Rockies, these species are truly adaptive.	withstand up to -60 degrees Fahrenheit without suffering serious winter injury. Riparia varieties are ideal for creating hardy hybrids. However, the cultivars tend to bloom early in the year but ripen late in the season.

PLANTING GRAPES

Make sure you have your entire vineyard ready before you begin planting. We discussed how to get soil sampling, adding fertilizer to improve levels of nutrients and row spacing should be done so make sure they are completed before you attempt your first planting.

ORDERING GRAPES

You will need to order your grape stock well in advance of starting your vineyard. In fact, some will need to be ordered up to 24 months prior to the planting so make sure you understand the wait time for the variant that you are selecting.

You will want to work with a rooted cutting for your very first planting as this will be much easier to get started and keep going. They should be at least a year old and you should ensure that the stocks are thoroughly inspected before planting. They should be approximately 3/8 of an inch around or thinner with the main stem only about the size of a pen.

The roots need to be moist and damp but not wet and definitely not dry. This is a sign that the plant will not survive so make sure you're looking for a healthy root system. If there are any problems with your delivery you will want to contact the supplier immediately for replacements.

PRUNING YOUR STOCKS

You will want to trim you stocks down before you plant them so they are healthy and grow properly. This requires you to trim to one sturdy stem with three to four active buds but no more. If there are any shoots growing make sure to clip them carefully. If you can't immediately plant them then make sure your stocks are stored somewhere cool and dry and are carefully misted and kept moist until you can plant.

If you have cold storage you can put the cuttings in that space though you will want to keep them above the freezing temperature. If you don't have this option then create a trench in the vineyard where there will be shade and cover the roots with organic mulch. This will provide the plants with nutrients while they wait for the planting. You'll also need to ensure that they have plenty of air circulation at this time.

Temporary planting can be much easier with a hydraulic auger since regular augers tend to produce too large of holes. You will want small, neat, loose holes for these cuttings rather than glazed holes.

PLANTING TIME

Your choices range from mechanical planting equipment to manually planting each stock. If you are in a hurry and wish to use less labor you could use mechanical planting. One thing you should know is that many vineyard owners have noted that these methods tend to produce inaccurate row spacing. Others state that it depends on the equipment used to determine whether this method will work for row spacing.

Make sure you keep your root systems moist during the entire planting process no matter which type you choose. You don't want them to get too dry as this will decrease your survival rate. While planting you have two options to do this:

- Submerge the roots in buckets
- Cover the stocks with a tarp to slow down evaporation

PRESERVING ROOTS

Make sure your holes are large enough to hold the cane and the entire root system. You don't want to hurt the roots because this will decrease the chance for survival of the vine. You also don't want to continue pruning at this point as it can also cause negative effects on the growth of your cuttings.

Spread the roots out carefully as you putting the cutting inside the hole you have made. You don't want them crumpled or buried in one spot at the bottom. They should be spread out manually so that they will spread out as the plant grows. Make sure you put soil around those roots and that you immediately water the plant.

SPRING PLANTING

The best time to plant your grapes is during early spring. Right after that winter frost has gone away you will have the best luck with your plants. Make sure the frost really is gone however as a spring frost could hurt your plants as well.

You will want to have the irrigation system and trellis system ready for your vineyard before you begin planting. You may decide to put off the trellis system until after your planting to create accurate spacing though many recommend this be done prior to the planting.

Once you've started your planting you'll want to check the soil around your canes. If there is a depression around the plant then it means you need more soil. You want the soil to be firmly packed and it must be level across the field. If you don't level out the soil around your cane you could end up with pooling of fertilizers and water around the plant which could kill it off.

FALL PLANTING

You can plant some hardy vines during the fall though this is generally not recommended. If you have summer cultivars then you definitely don't want to plant them at this time as they won't be strong enough to withstand the colder weather. Of course there are some other reasons that planting at this time of year is generally not preferred such as nurseries not being ready with the cultivar.

You will want to ensure that you are ordering well in advance if you are going to get cuttings for the fall planting. They should also be in a dormant condition when you plant which means they will be stored in cold storage. Make sure you also protect your vines from frost and that you are not overwatering them since they do not need as much water during this season.

THE FIRST TWO YEARS

Make sure that for the first two years you are protecting your vines from insects. You will need to keep fertilizers at a proper level as well so that you don't have additional problems with low nutrients in your soil.

ORGANIC FARMING AND DISEASE

One of the biggest problems with vineyards is called vine disease which can occur from bacteria or fungi. This will transfer to different vines of different cultivars and species so it is especially important to watch out for.

European Vinifera-European cultivars can cause problems when planted on American soil because it reduces their natural resistances. These are not as resistant to pests and diseases when planted on American soil and may suffer from black rot. It's important to utilize proper application of fungicides in order to prevent this.

American Species-Native American cultivars are not any more resistant to pests either. In fact, some of them may have as much or more trouble with these diseases. Some cultivars will be resistant to black rot or other molds but insects are still a problem.

If you want a disease resistant plant you may want to check into Norton and Edelweiss cultivars. These are much better are resisting fungal and bacterial disease.

Managing disease however can be difficult for those who are looking to continue an organic method of planting and maintaining their harvest. You will want to look into fungicides and herbicides anyway as these can be much better for getting rid of bug problems and disease. Some of the most 'organic' forms of these are made from sulfur however this should be used with care. If it accumulates on the plant it can cause tissue damage as well as killing off helpful insects.

If you're going to use these types of fungicides you'll want to choose a plant that can stand up to sulfur. You will likely need to utilize this product quite regularly at some point during the season and if you don't have a hardy plant it will have problems with this product.

ABOUT THE AUTHOR

Hello everyone! My name is Bowe Chaim Packer and I am a bit of a wacky, zany, fun loving guy who does his best to constantly wear his heart out on his sleeve. I must say though, like many of you might already know, it often is challenging in this world that we live in.

Throughout the years I have come to realize the only thing that I can truly be in control of is me. Or shall I say my actions and how I show up in the world. For me it is all about taking responsibility for how I act, how I treat myself and how I treat others. Wheewwwww, and I won't lie, sometimes it takes everything I have to make a decision to act appropriately.

When I do, things always seem to turn out as they should. Funny how that works.!.! ;-)

So, here I am publishing information to the world for consumption. I hope whatever words your read of mine and in whatever format you choose to read them in, that they make a difference in your life. No matter how small or large that difference maybe, it will tell me (in a cosmic kind of way) that I have done my job......

Be sure to always keep your heart open and listening with great intent, for then and only then, you will find what you are looking for in that moment.

Remember, LIFE is a journey for each and every one of us. We must never forget the things that are important to us or lose sight of what makes us happy.

A FEW BOOKS BY ME (see author link below for my

complete portfolio)

Antiquing Secrets: Fastest Way To Discover Antique History & Learn How To Collect Antiques Like A Seasoned Veteran

Click on the link to check it out on Kindle:

http://amzn.to/1r2De8t

Aquaponics System: A Practical Guide To Building And Maintaining Your Own Backyard Aquaponics

Click on the link to check it out on Kindle:

http://amzn.to/1yo4oco

Probiotics: A Practical Guide To The Benefits Of Probiotics And Your Health

Click on the link to check it out on Kindle:

http://amzn.to/1t0aBZ9

Astral Travel: Your Guide To Understanding Astral Projection & The Effective & Safe Astral Travel Techniques

Click on the link to check it out on Kindle:

http://amzn.to/1jvDXy3

"Terrible Twos": Stopping Toddler Tantrums and

Toddler Behavior Problems Quickly

Click on the link to check it out on Kindle:

http://amzn.to/1t0cJzQ

MY COMPLETE PORTFOLIO

Click on the link to check out my complete portfolio:

http://amzn.to/1tOkOM9

Includes all formats – paperback, digital (Kindle) and audio for your convenience and preference.

Questions for me?

Email me @: bowe@sunshineinmysoul.net

AND JUST ONE LAST THING BEFORE WE PART OUR WAYS.....

In life I am coming to understand if you don't ask for what you want, then there is truly no chance of you ever getting it.

With that said, if you are on a Kindle reader, when you turn the page, Kindle will give you an opportunity to rate the book and share your thoughts.

If you believe that your friends, other followers and new readers alike would get something valuable from this book, I would be **honored** if you posted your thoughts.

Also, if you feel particularly strong about the contributions this book made to your life in any way, I would be **eternally grateful** if you posted a review on Amazon. Just go back to your orders within Amazon and click on *"Write a Product Review"* next to the book.

And if you are not on a Kindle reader and would still like to post an Amazon review, well then I would be **delighted, grateful and extremely happy**......

Here is a link to my authors page on Amazon if you are having a hard time trying to find where to leave your review:

Bowe Packer
http://amzn.to/1tOkOM9

Once on my authors page you can click on the book you want to leave a review on and then scroll down until you see the button *"write a customer review"*.
This would also help me learn how I can better serve my readers.

In Gratitude,

Bowe Chaim Packer

Ingram Content Group UK Ltd.
Milton Keynes UK
UKHW021320260623
424060UK00019B/436